How To Pray the ROSARY

For Your FAMILY

Dr. Paul J. Young

DEDICATION: This book is dedicated to:

1. All readers who have committed themselves to pray the Rosary for their family. The world needs more of you!

2. All those who have a family member or friend praying the Rosary for them. What a blessing to have such a relative or friend! Thank God for them.

3. The many family members and friends I pray for each day including my wife, sons, daughter, fourteen grandchildren, brothers, cousins, along with many friends and neighbors. I love you and want God's best for you!

A <u>DRPAULYOUNG.COM</u> **publication**

Read This First

No one discards a box of delicious fried chicken because it has bones. No way! You grab a piece, eat the meat and discard the bones.

So too with this book. Eat the meat - there is a lot here to chew on, think about, process and pray about. If you find any bones, discard them. Why waste all the meat because there are a few bones! (No book authored by a human is perfect, you know).

Most of all, why not use this book of prayers to change your life and the lives of others?

Read. Drink in the principles.

Pray. Blast through a prayer-less-ness that is crippling many families, maybe your own life.

Reap a great harvest with a life or many lives changed through your powerful, Holy Spirit guided prayers.

Bravo!

Contents

How To Use This Book To Pray For Family

If you bought this book to be used as a guide to pray for your family, I encourage you to use it regularly.

When we pray for family members, we often don't know how to pray, specifically, powerfully and purposely. There are many cases where you will not see a family member for a month, a year or even longer. There may even be times where there is a rift between a family member where you are estranged. Yet, you can still pray in a way that will change their lives. The Holy Spirit can take what you say, speak to that person you are praying for, even though you can't speak to them, and make a difference.

What are the needs of a family member? How should you pray prayers for them that will allow the Holy Spirit to work in their lives?

This book will guide you so that you can pray...

- Specifically
- Purposefully
- Powerfully

Remember, PRAYER CHANGES NOT JUST THINGS, BUT PEOPLE.   As you pray for a family member, you could actually…

Spark a SPIRITUAL REVOLUTION in their lives!

Change a person
Change a family
Change the world!

DON'T JUST *SAY* THE ROSARY
PRAY THE ROSARY

Saint Dominic was encouraged by our Blessed Mother to bring about changes in his society by praying THROUGH Mary to Jesus. The power that came through these prayers was not just the focus on our Blessed Mother, Mary, but also on the Mysteries that were the focus on each day, Mysteries that would teach those who meditated on them the content of their faith.

In one sense, all one needs to know about their Christian faith is the whole of the Rosary - the Apostles creed and the Mysteries. To meditate on these, to plunder the depth of them is to enter into the rich heritage of our faith, taking us deep into the person of Mary and Jesus, into the throne room of God where our prayers are being heard.

IT IS A POWERFUL ACTION THAT WE ARE DOING!

It must be noted too that we should not just say the Rosary but PRAY the Rosary.

Prayer is not a one sided talk with God. It should be a dialogue where we speak and allow time for listening. There are many who say the Rosary, recite it each day in a rote way and are done with it.

Though this is not bad in itself, we all can say the Rosary more powerfully and intentionally for our families and friends. As we do so, we are grabbing the attention of Mary and the powerful assistance of Jesus Christ our Lord. We enter the Holy of Holies and are communing with them.

Let's do our best not to rush through these holy moments. And instead of SAYING the Rosary, PRAY it, our hearts open to meditation and contemplation as we spend time in the presence of Jesus and his mother, Mary.

Pope Paul VI clearly points out the right way to pray the Rosary when he says:

> *Without contemplation, the Rosary is a body without a soul, and its recitation runs the risk of becoming a mechanical repetition of formulas in violation of the admonition of Christ, 'In praying do not heap up empty phrases as the Gentiles do; for they think they will be heard for their many words.'*

> Matthew 6:7

He goes on to say that:

> *We should make every effort to meditate on the Mysteries each and every time we pray the Rosary. The Rosary is no substitute for Lectio Divina* (a prayerful reading of Scripture)*; on the contrary, it presupposes and promotes it.*

As you pray the Rosary, be open to God's voice as you talk with him. He wants to carry on a conversation with you. And he will do this as you pray the Rosary for each family member or friend. He will stop you, at times, make you slow down and help you to pray specific, powerful requests as you intercede for a family member or friend. This means REAL PRAYER will be happening - not just you doing all the talking. You will be dialoguing with God as you pray through the Rosary.

In this book, we are focusing on PRAYING the Rosary for a FAMILY MEMBER or members. As we pray, we are bringing them to Mary as she brings them before Jesus who loves us and continues to give us his best.

In the truest sense, you are fulfilling your responsibility as a PRIEST of your family (the common priesthood of all Christians) as you mediate for them with your Holy Mother.

What a HOLY TASK you have! And through the in-living Holy Spirit…

You Can Do It!

Your Prayer...for your Family

Write down below a list of all the people
you are praying for each day.

Family members: Wife, husband, sons, daughters, parents, brothers,
sisters, grandparents, aunts, uncles, cousins, grandchildren, in-laws, nephews, nieces

1.	19.
2.	20.
3.	21.
4.	22.
5.	23.
6.	24.
7.	25.
8.	26.
9.	27.
10.	28.
11.	29.
12.	30.
13.	31.
14.	32.
15.	33.
16.	34.
17.	35.
18.	36.

Prayer.

What an awesome gift it is.

Imagine if a hero of yours, or some famous world leader or Hollywood personality called you and wanted to set up an appointment to meet with you each day. That would blow your socks off!

Well, you have been invited by the CEO of the universe, God himself, to meet with him each day and talk, not just to monologue, but to dialogue with him about many things, things dear to him and to you.

One of the things you should always talk with him about is **YOUR FAMILY**. They should be are on your mind every day. So when you pray, you will talk with God about your family and intercede for them.

Because you are not in touch with them as often as you'd like, you don't know all the hopes and dreams they have as well as the difficulties they face. Yet that is not a problem because you cover just about everything you need in your prayers.

Though they might be pursuing things that will not in the end bring happiness, your prayers for them focus on what they really want and desire - an inward peace and joy that will put them at ease with themselves and the world around them.

This peace (freedom from anxiety) and joy (an inward happiness that is not based on friends or things but on God) is what they ultimately long for.

You want them to have this wish come true - for them to truly live happily ever after, now and in the life to come.

Too often we all forget that we are ultimately souls that dwell in a body specially designed by God. In this day it is easy to forget that and focus on the body and all its needs - to run after money, recognition and pleasure forgetting that it is only in the presence of God that we can have true pleasure.

King David said:

> *You will show me the path to life*
> *Abounding joy in your presence*
> *The delights of your right hand*
> *Forever.*
>
> Psalm 16:11

Why then do we all resist this time with God, this appointment to spend in his presence drinking up his light, life and love?

One of the reasons you pray for your family each day is that they would open themselves to HIS PRESENCE, not in some churchy way, but in a way that brings a new reality into their lives, the reality of the Living God!

Billions of people have lived before them trudging along, NEVER FINDING THE SATISFACTION THEIR HEARTS LONG FOR. Why should they follow in their path - searching, longing, when they can come to the living water that will quench their inner being...

THEIR SOUL!

So you pray for them, SPECIFIC PRAYERS, prayers that ask God to keep them from wandering too far and bring them into his eternal home.

These specific prayers follow an old tradition that has gone on for hundreds of years. Through most of human history, people didn't know how to read. So this ancient prayer was developed to teach people about the movements of the life of Christ and the gospel without having to read.

It's called the Rosary.

Picture of Rosary from:

PRAYING THE ROSARY AND MEDITATING ON THE MYSTERIES

By Rev. John Trigilio, Rev. Kenneth Brighenti

Catholicism For Dummies, 3rd Edition

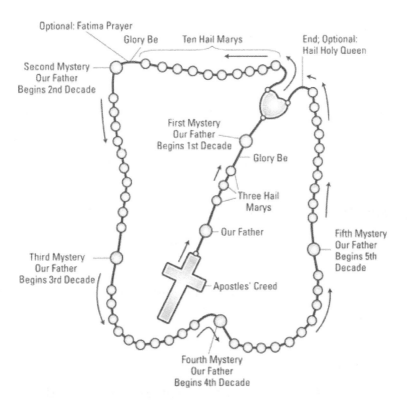

The normal sequence of praying through the Rosary:

- Make the sign of the Cross
- The Apostles Creed
- The Our Father
- 3 Hail Mary's
- The Glory Be
- Say each Mystery followed by:
- The Our Father
- 10 Hail Marys
- The Glory Be
- The Fatima Prayer
- The Hail Holy Queen at the end of the five Mysteries for that day
- Concluding Prayer

You've seen them.

You hopefully have one tucked away somewhere.

These beads on the Rosary, if followed, move us to pray in specific, guided ways each day.

Long before the Rosary was developed, monks tied knots into a small rope with each knot reminding them what prayer they should pray. Later they made beads tied together to assist them. Soon they began to call these beads and the prayers, the Rosary. Why? Mary, our blessed Mother, is often associated with the rose because of its beauty and smell.[1]

There are many stories where the smell of roses have noted Mary's presence.

When St. Juan Diego talked with Mary in Mexico hundreds of years ago (Our Lady of Guadalupe), she directed him to some roses so he could take them to his Bishop and thus prove he had seen the Blessed Mother…roses growing in the frozen ground in the dead of winter! Impossible! Yet verified and true.

Though we pray to Mary as we say the Rosary, we are really praying THOUGH her to Jesus. Even as we ask a friend or

[1]Most perfumes today are made out of a small amount rose oil - so rich and awesome the smell! It costs thousands of dollars an ounce. Years ago when I worked in Bulgaria, a place that produces 90% of world supply of rose oil, an ounce sold for $10,000!

relative to remember us in prayer, we are asking Mary, the Blessed Mother of the God-man Jesus, to pray for us. After all, she knows Jesus her son better than anyone. Like the Queen mothers in the days of Israel's kingdom, Mary has a special place with her son, won by God's grace, to speak to Jesus on our behalf.

It is true that we can go directly to Jesus at anytime. And we should! But to have additional support in our prayers, to have holy forces standing with us, heavenly forces that have won the victory and pray that we would also win the prize of eternal life, is the kind of support we desperately need.

So you pray this ancient prayer for your family, the Rosary, consisting of Scripture found in Luke 2, as well as an addition added in the 4th century. It is a very old prayer prayed by many of the early Christians and continues as millions pray this every day.

Hail Mary, full of grace, the Lord is with thee,
Blessed art thou among women and
Blessed is the fruit of thy womb, Jesus.
Holy Mary, Mother of God,
Pray for us sinners now,
and at the hour of our death. Amen.

It was hundreds of years later that the MYSTERIES were added to this ancient prayer. These mysteries (deep truths) take us on a journey through God's mission to save the human race from self seeking to God seeking and loving others.

They are prayers even prayed by some Protestant reformers who had a far higher view of Mary than most modern Protestants.   Some even used the Rosary, as did Martin Luther, who prayed to and through Mary to Jesus.   He knew of her special place as the Mother of God - Jesus Christ our redeemer.[2]

---

[2] See David Armstrong and his article on the web entitled, *Martin Luther's Devotion to Mary*. If you are a Protestant, you may not agree with *HOW* I pray but appreciate and embrace most of *WHAT* I pray. They are prayers that go wide and deep having a breadth and depth than many prayers lack.

There are FOUR MYSTERIES

Each mystery has 5 parts

1. The JOYFUL Mysteries

1) **The Annunciation** - *Angel to Mary* - Luke 1

2) **The Visitation** - *Mary with Elizabeth* - Luke 1

3) **The Nativity** - *Bethlehem the birth of Jesus* - Luke 2

4) **The Presentation** -*The babe Jesus taken to the Temple* -
   Luke 2

5) **Finding Jesus in the Temple** - Luke 2

2. The SORROWFUL Mysteries

1) **Agony** in the garden - Matthew 26

2) **Scourging** at the pillar - John 19

3) **Crowning** with thorns - Matthew 27

4) **Carrying** the cross - John 19

5) **Crucifixion** - Matthew 27

3. The GLORIOUS Mysteries

1) **The Resurrection** - Matthew 28

2) **The Ascension** - Matthew 28

3) **Descent of the Holy Spirit** - Acts 2

4) **Assumption of Mary**[3] - Luke 2

5) **Coronation of Mary** - Revelation 12

---

[3]In early Church teaching, God's grace (the angel said she was FULL of grace) preserved Mary when conceived in her mother's womb so she would have a prefect vessel to give birth to the God-man, Jesus Christ. Therefore her body at death was not corrupted by sin and as a result was received into God's presence to stand by her son, Jesus, and pray for us. Martin Luther and other early Protestant leaders supported this teaching.

4. The **LUMINOUS** Mysteries

1) **Baptism of Jesus** - *Sacrament of Baptism* - John 1, 3, Acts 2

2) **Feast at Cana** - *Sacrament of Marriage* - John 2

3) **Preaching the Kingdom** - *Sacrament of Reconciliation and Last Rites* - Mark 1, John 20, James 5

4) **The Transfiguration** - *Sacrament of Confirmation and Holy Orders* - Luke 9, Acts 8, I Tim. 3

5) **The Eucharist** - *The Blessed Sacrament - John 6, I Corinthians 10 -11*

That means that when you **pray for them...**

1. You will make **5 SPECIFIC REQUESTS** for your family EACH DAY tied to each Mystery, and they vary over the period of four days with some repeated to complete the week.

2. Therefore you will pray a total of **20 SPECIFIC, UNIQUE REQUESTS** for your family EACH WEEK, requests that God hears. You will see them listed later and the specific things you pray for, things we all need in our lives, prayers that will release God's power to bring about the peace and joy your family desires.

3. Before all this, you make the sign of the Cross and then recite the Apostles Creed, say the Our Father, three Hail Marys and then the Glory Be. As you say these, you are praying also for YOUR FAMILY specifically, prayers that surround them in all that they are and do.

These prayers of yours will make a difference. Though family members may stray from the Lord at times, these prayers will arrest the attention of the Holy Spirit who will also NUDGE THEM to live for God and let their soul be filled with his presence.

So...on with your prayers FOR YOUR FAMILY!

Guided Daily Prayers For

YOUR FAMILY!

And your response

Come. Read through these prayers you pray for YOUR FAMILY each day and...

Pray them too for yourself.

If you give yourself to these prayers that you pray for your family you could very well find a peace and joy that you've never had before as you trust your family into Mary's and Jesus' care.

It's sure worth a try, isn't it!

Your first prayer each day for

YOUR FAMILY

You begin by making the SIGN OF THE CROSS and say:

I pray for my family (mention their names)

In the Name of the

Father, Son, and the Holy Spirit. Amen.

One way you express your daily need for Christ as an individual as well as for your family is to make the sign of the cross picturing THEM in your mind. The cross of Christ brings freedom and grace. It has the power to transform us. Therefore, when you make the sign of the cross throughout the day - not only when you pray before meals, but at other times of prayer, you are asking God to save you, to transform you, to mark you as his own.

Normally the sign of the cross begins by touching our foreheads - our minds, given to Christ. Then the sign moves to our hearts - all of us, our souls given to Christ. Then we move to both sides of our lungs, our breath, the breath God gave us, all of it given to him, our creator, our sustainer, our LORD and our God.

The REAL POWER of the cross is the PERSON who died for us, who lives in us, who wants us to take our cross and follow him. HE is the real power, and that power is released in us as we take up that cross and sacrificially give our lives for God and others.

So as you make the sign of the cross over yourself and each member of your family, you identify yourself and them with Jesus. You mark THEM with HIS SPECIAL, LOVING, SACRIFICIAL MARK.

As I said before, there is great power released as we make the sign of the cross over ourselves. It allows God's power to be released in our lives as we trust in Christ who died and gave himself for us.

Again, you do this for YOUR FAMILY.

Alexander Solzhenitsyn, the great Russian thinker, writer and Christian, talked about the time when he had lost all hope of ever getting out of the brutal suffering he was going through each day in the Soviet prison camp. Day after day he worked in the fields, in the rain, in the snow, through the hard winters, backbreaking work that was more than he could bear. This intense suffering reduced him to a state of absolute despair. Depression swept over him, a hopelessness so dominated his soul that he was ready to quit. There was no reason to keep going. What good could this suffering do? What value would come from his torture?

So he gave up.

Leaving his shovel on the ground, Solzhenitsyn walked over to a crude bench, sat down and waited for the guard to shout at him to keep on working. When he failed to get up, the guard would beat him to death, probably with the shovel he had dropped by his side. He had seen that happen so many times to other prisoners. It would surely happen to him.

With his head down, he felt the presence of someone by his side. Slowly Solzhenitsyn looked up and saw a skinny old prisoner squat down. He said nothing. Instead, with a crooked stick, traced the sign of the cross and then returned to his work.

As Solzhenitsyn stared at the cross drawn in the dirt, he felt something happening in his soul. Life was returning. The hope that had faded was becoming bright again. All the evil of the Soviet empire was nothing in light of the cross - the CROSS OF JESUS, the cross that conquered the world. With the cross, anything was possible.

Solzhenitsyn slowly rose to his feet, picked up his shovel and went back to work. It appeared on the outside that nothing had changed. But a miracle had just occurred in the heart of a defeated man. A smile splashed across his face as he faced the horrific conditions with hope, with a Jesus who knew how to suffer, and in suffering, triumphed.

> *God forbid that I should glory save in the CROSS of our LORD JESUS CHRIST.*
>
> St. Paul, Galatians 6:14

This is why you mark yourself and your family with the cross. It has power to heal, to cleanse, to liberate and to bring triumph.

YOUR RESPONSE TO THE PRAYER YOU PRAY FOR YOUR FAMILY

Yes, LORD. I cross myself now with the sign of the cross, a sign that I make willingly with a renewed commitment to follow you, my Lord and my God.

Amen.

After you make the Sign of the Cross,

you pray

The Apostles Creed

This creed was used as early as the 2nd century and is an early statement of Christian belief. As you recite this creed, you are praying for YOUR FAMILY (use their names) that they will not only believe it, but live out its truth in their lives.

I pray that my family would

Believe

in God, the Father Almighty, Creator of Heaven and earth;

I pray that my family would

Believe

in Jesus Christ, His only Son Our Lord, Who was conceived by the Holy Spirit, born of the Virgin Mary, suffered under Pontius Pilate, was crucified, died, and was buried. He descended into Hell; the third day He rose again from the dead; He ascended into Heaven, and is seated at the right hand of God, the Father almighty; from there He shall come to judge the living and the dead.

I pray that my family would

Believe

in the Holy Spirit, the holy Catholic Church, the communion of saints, the forgiveness of sins, the resurrection of the body and life everlasting.

Amen.

YOUR RESPONSE TO THE PRAYER YOU PRAY
FOR YOUR FAMILY

Yes, LORD.   I embrace the Apostles Creed and seek to not only believe it, but live out its truth in my life.

Amen.

Next you pray the **OUR FATHER**

This is one of the greatest prayers
you can say every day as you pray it for
YOUR FAMILY.

Our Father,
Who art in heaven
Hallowed be…
Thy Name;
Thy Kingdom come,
Thy Will be done,
on earth as it is in heaven.
Give us this day our daily bread, and
Forgive us our trespasses,
as we forgive those who trespass against us; and
Lead us not into temptation, but
Deliver us from evil. Amen.

As you pray this prayer for your FAMILY, you pray to God that…

THY NAME

1. They would **reverence** the God who made and loves them. May they be able to call him their "Father."

THY KINGDOM

2. They would live for God's **Kingdom** and not their own. May they have a longing in their heart for God's thoughts and ways and seek first the "kingdom of God and his righteousness."

THY WILL

3. They would **submit THEIR WILL** to him seeking God's will and not their own. May they be submissive to God in every thing they do and say.

GIVE US

4. They will THANK GOD for all their **daily provisions.** May God take care of all their physical, emotional and spiritual needs today. And may they see the value of taking the Eucharist as food for their soul.

FORGIVE US

5. They accept God's grace, mercy and **forgiveness**. And may they have a heart full of forgiveness for others particularly those who have hurt them. May God save them from resentment and bitterness and may they shower those they live with, with God's love.

LEAD US

6. They will not give in to **TEMPTATION** particularly those sins that seem habitual. That they will let God LEAD them as he tests them with many trials that are common to life (see I Cor. 10:13). His tests are never temptations to sin but rather trials to see if we will be faithful to him and take his escape route from sin and failure and thus find victory, hope and joy.

DELIVER US

7. They will **be aware that the evil one**, Satan and his army is out to destroy them, but God seeks to give them victory over them. May THEY run from temptation and find the joy of victory through the deliverance that the Holy Spirit can bring.

Amen.

YOUR RESPONSE TO THIS PRAYER THAT YOU PRAY FOR YOUR FAMILY

Yes, LORD. I choose to also pray the OUR FATHER, using the word "our" to show that I am a participating part of your great family.

As I hallow your name, desire to live for your Kingdom and submit myself to your perfect will, I am confident that you will honor that commitment and give me daily provisions, forgiveness for my sins and power to escape any test or temptation that comes my way.

Thank you my Father for who you are and your constant love for me as you take care of my every need.

Amen.

Then you **pray the Hail Mary**

asking Mary to talk with her son

for YOUR FAMILY

Hail Mary,
Full of grace,
the Lord is with thee,
Blessed art thou among women and
Blessed is the fruit of thy womb,
Jesus.

Holy Mary,
Mother of God,
Pray for us sinners ... now
and at the hour of our death.
Amen.

This historic prayer made to Mary by the early Church talks about her special GRACE.

St. Luke in his gospel said that she was **FULL OF GRACE** - a word used only one time in the Bible to describe this special favor given to her by God. This fullness left no room for sin!

Yet it is also God's desire to fill us all with his grace, to push out any sin, any shortcoming and make us whole and perfect. You pray that your family would become FULL of God's grace, filled up totally so that there is no room for anything else but God.

Mary is called, "**Mother of God**."

There was debate in the early days of the Church whether she was mother of Jesus or mother of God.

It took until the 3RD CENTURY to *fully ascertain who Jesus was* - fully God and fully man.

After the Holy Spirit led the Church to state this clearly in the Nicene Creed, they moved on to debate who Mary was, the blessed mother of Jesus.

It was in the 4TH CENTURY (Council of Ephesus in AD 431) that it was declared that she was the *Mother of God,* not primarily to make her look so great, but to protect the one she bore, the GOD-man Jesus Christ, declaring that he was not just a man, but God, and if God, it meant that Mary was the Mother of God.

You pray that today, your family, like Mary, would allow this GOD-man to be birthed in their lives, to the glory of God. Amen.

As you pray the Hail Mary, your desire is for Mary to pray to Jesus **NOW**...today, at this hour in all the circumstances your family may face. As a mother, she loves your family and wants her son to be there for them...NOW!

Then you want your heavenly mother to pray for your family at the hour of their death. Why? She wants to bring them into the presence of her son, Jesus.

It is a holy thing when the people of God die. And it is a blessing that they have a holy, heavenly mother who is there to assure that the journey from death to eternal life with Jesus will happen. What a blessing and gift this is for all of us... especially for your family!

YOUR RESPONSE TO THE PRAYER YOU PRAY
FOR YOUR FAMILY

Yes, LORD. I submit myself to Mary's prayers for me. And even as you, Jesus, in a unique way, mediate my salvation, thank you that my Holy Mother mediates, interceding with you about my spiritual growth so that I might be more like you, Lord Jesus. May I be filled with grace, filled with you, Lord Jesus, full and running over with your love.

Reduce me to love!

Amen.

After this you pray the **"GLORY BE."**

As you pray it, you are praying that your family would live each day not to glorify themselves, but God. The more they seek to bring glory to themselves, the more unhappy they will be…guaranteed.

Look at all those around you that seek their desires first, who want the world to focus on themselves. Yes, they may get a lot of accolades, status and money, but in the end, their lives wind up on the trash heap, suffering from constant boredom, meaninglessness, anxiety, depression, stress, and anger. This spiral downwards often results in failed relationships and marriages, drug addiction and even suicide.

When your family lives to bring attention to God and others, their hearts will experience a fulfillment that they cannot find anywhere else. They will be truly satisfied DEEP WITHIN. And this is what you pray for, this deep, overflowing joy that will bubble from their souls.

THE GLORY BE...

GLORY BE to the Father, the Son, and the Holy Spirit. As it was in the beginning, is now and ever shall be, world without end. Amen.

This is a prayer of victory and triumph. Your prayer for your family can result in this victory, a victory that will "now and ever shall be…"

YOUR RESPONSE TO THE PRAYER YOU PRAY
FOR YOUR FAMILY

Yes, LORD. I want this victory, victory that flows from giving and bringing to you glory in every part of my life - physical, mental, emotional, social and spiritual.

Amen.

Then You Pray…

THE FATIMA PRAYER

After you pray the 5 Mysteries each day, you close with the prayer of Fatima. Mary appeared to three young children at Fatima and encouraged them to lead people in repentance of sin. She asked them to pray…

Oh my Jesus, forgive us our sins, save us from the fires of hell, and lead all souls to Heaven, especially those most in need of Thy Mercy.

Amen.

Our Lady of Fatima, July 13, 1917

When you pray this prayer, you pause when you say the word, "sins," and confess to God your own sins.

As you ask Jesus to save your family from the fires of hell, you will pray this specifically for each member of your family. Your prayers for them as well as your prayers for others will release the power of God by helping your family and friends escape hell and go to heaven.

In all of our Blessed Mother's communication at Fatima and Lourdes, she states that many go straight to hell when they die. This is a frightful thought that some of your family would go to a place of eternal doom. This is why you pray. You stand with Job (the book of Job in the Old Testament) who made daily sacrifices for his children.

> *Job would...sanctify them, rising early and offering burnt sacrifices for every one of his children, for Job said, "It may be that my sons have sinned and blasphemed God in their hearts. This Job did habitually.* Job 1: 5

Job was a righteous man who prayed for his family, DAILY. You choose to stand with Job to pray for your family that they might not go to hell, but find joy in the presence of God forever. Pray that they will be led to heaven in triumph and joy, entering the eternal city with praise on their lips and enjoy the presence and purpose of God forever.

As you remember those who are in most need of mercy, why don't you name those family members who need that...today.

Oh my Jesus,

    forgive my family our sins,

    save my family from the fires of hell
        and

    lead all my family to Heaven,

For we are all in need of

    Thy Mercy.

        Amen.

YOUR RESPONSE TO THE PRAYER YOU PRAY FOR YOUR FAMILY

Oh my Jesus, forgive me my sins. Save ME from the fires of hell, and lead my soul to heaven, for I am in most need of your mercy.

Amen.

Finally, after you pray the five Mysteries each day for YOUR FAMILY, you say the

Hail Holy Queen prayer.

Hail, Holy Queen, Mother of Mercy, our life, our sweetness, and our hope.

To you do we cry poor banished children of Eve.

To you do we send up our sighs, mourning, and weeping in this valley of tears.

Turn then, O most gracious advocate, your eyes of mercy toward my family, and after this our exile...

Show unto my family the blessed fruit of your womb, Jesus.

O clement! O loving! O sweet Virgin Mary!

Pray for my family, O Holy Mother of God. That we may be made worthy of the promises of Christ.

Insight and intentions of this
prayer that you make for
YOUR FAMILY

1. It is a prayer that recognizes that *Mary is a Queen.*

    In the Old Testament all the mothers of kings were called
    the Queen Mother. Since Mary is the mother of Jesus who
    is in the line of King David, and since Jesus is King, Mary
    too is a Queen, the Queen Mother.

    She is also called Holy because she is the Ark of God, a
    picture drawn from the Holy Ark Of The Covenant which
    held the Law and other holy elements in the Jewish
    Temple. Mary held the Holy Jesus in her womb which
    was a Holy Ark housing Jesus, the God-man.

    You pray for your family that they, like Mary, might also
    hold in their bodies and souls the person and life of Jesus
    Christ.

2. *Mary is called mother of mercy* because she is the mother
    of the merciful one, Jesus Christ, and from him flows this
    special grace.

3. Because *Holy Mary raised Jesus who is our life,
    sweetness and hope,* she is connected with these attributes
    too. From her womb she gave this life who can become

our life. You pray for your family that they might receive this life.

4. We cry to Mary because we were *banished from God due to the original sin* of Adam and Eve who were chased from the Garden of Eden. As we cry with sighs, mourning and weeping, we are showing outwardly our true repentance. May your family repent from sin, cry for and accept the mercy of Jesus Christ as their redeemer.

5. In the Old Testament we see *the Queen Mothers' pleading with their sons to show mercy to others.* Thus Mary as Queen Mother, pleads with her son to be merciful to us. Thank God for her pleadings! Though we deserve punishment for our temporal, everyday sins, (You do continue to sin, don't you!) she pleads for continued and ongoing mercy and grace. It is ours for the asking, won by Christ at the cross. May each family member pause and ask forgiveness for sins not confessed.

6. *Our exile in a fallen world will come to an end* through the mercy of Jesus as his merciful, gracious advocate, our Holy Mother, prays for us. She prays that we might experience resurrection and life in the new heavens and earth, free from all the disarray caused by sin. It is in this new existence bought by Christ's death that we will be with HIM our LORD and Savior.

Our Holy Mother Mary will show us her Son like we've never seen him before. WE SHALL BEHOLD **HIM** in all his glory and majesty, in stunning brilliance, holiness, and unmatched love and grace…FOREVER. This is the goal of our Blessed Mother's prayers…for us! May your family experience this awesome goal.

7. *O Clement*…means merciful, O loving…what love! O sweet Virgin Mary…pure, holy, prepared especially to give birth and to raise the God-man, Jesus, and to pray for us at his side.

8. Last, we conclude this prayer to Holy Mary by asking her to pray for us, even as we do in the Hail Marys, that we may *finish our course here on earth,* and finish well.

   You pray for each family member that they may be finishers.

9. *Made worthy*…No one can make themselves worthy. To think so is nonsense! All humankind is saved ONLY THROUGH GOD'S GRACE…not of works that we can boast. Yet we are to cooperate with Christ even as St. Paul said: *Work out your salvation with fear and trembling…for it is God who is at work in you giving you the will and desire to do his work.* (Philippians 2:12-13). It is this grace of God that inhabits us and allows us to do works that make us worthy.

May your family not trust in their own work, but in the work of Christ in them, an evidence of his grace.

YOUR RESPONSE TO THE PRAYER YOU PRAY
FOR YOUR FAMILY

Yes LORD. I need your Mother's prayers for me so that I may experience your grace to counter my sins and thereby spend an eternity in your glorious presence.

Amen.

Your Concluding Prayer
for YOUR FAMILY!

O God,

Whose only-begotten Son, by His
    life,
    death and
    resurrection,
has purchased for my family
the rewards of eternal life;

Grant, I beseech Thee,
    that, *meditating* upon these mysteries of
    the Most Holy Rosary of the Blessed
Virgin Mary,

I and my family may
    imitate what they contain and
    obtain what they promise,

Through the same Christ our Lord.

                Amen.

There are **FOUR MYSTERIES** that you cover in your prayers for your family each week. Each mystery has 5 parts.

The
JOYFUL
Mysteries

I. JOYFUL MYSTERIES

Monday & Saturday

Today we focus on joy as we pray through the Rosary. God is finally going to fulfill a promise of sending his Son to redeem humankind, a promise made to Adam and Eve in Genesis 3:15 when he said that "through the seed of the woman" this redeemer would come, overthrow Satan and bring recovery to the human race.

In the Joyful Mysteries we see it happening right before our eyes. The Redeemer is coming through that woman promised thousands of years earlier. She will become the Ark of God and have the holy privilege of bringing God incarnate into the world. She is the New Eve, the Blessed One, our Mother, Mary.

What a gift she is. What a gift she brings to the world, Jesus Christ our Lord. And what JOY is ours!

Joy to the world the Lord is come!

1. The Annunciation of the Lord to Mary

The angel said: "Hail Mary full of grace,
the Lord is with you." Luke 1

Today, God, I pray for my family that they, like Mary, would be full of your grace, that special favor and kindness that only you can give. Release in them the spiritual beauty of all of your graces. May they, with our Holy Mother, experience your presence, right now, (God with them) in everything they do.

Keep them aware of the presence of Jesus, your son, and may they commune with him today, the God who loves them and wants to fill them with grace, peace, hope and love, as well as total and complete fulfillment and satisfaction.

Holy Mary, ask Jesus to be especially kind to my family today and let them know that no matter wherever they are in life, they can always find forgiveness and blessing in the presence of Jesus, your son.

Inhabit my family today. May your son, Jesus, come, live in them and be their Lord and Savior in a very personal way. And may his presence protect them and keep them safe and pure.

May the beauty and elegance of God be upon my family, an inward beauty and elegance of soul that will show forth the grace of God to others at home, at work, at school, or wherever they might be.

As my family sits down for a meal, may they say "grace," knowing that all good things come from the hand of God who loves them.

Finally, Holy Mary, pray for my family as you talk with your son, Jesus. May they not live in condemnation but under the shadow of the GRACE, kindness and generosity of Christ their Savior.

Amen.

To reinforce this mystery Pray the Our Father, ten Hail Marys, the Glory Be and the Fatima Prayer

YOUR RESPONSE TO THE PRAYER YOU PRAY
FOR YOUR FAMILY

Yes, LORD. I do desire to be filled with your grace today… clear to the brim, up and running over. May I not only receive this grace from you, but offer it to others around me, people who need to experience this special grace from you.

Amen.

2. The Visitation of Mary to Elizabeth

When Mary visited her cousin Elizabeth,
Elizabeth's baby leaped in her womb and she cried aloud,
moved by the Holy Spirit:
Of all women you are most blessed and blessed is the fruit
of your womb (Jesus). Luke 1

Though you were pregnant, Mary, you went to help your cousin. I pray, Holy Mary that my family will learn to have this same humble quality, to be helpers, to learn how to serve with generosity and love.

Holy Mary, may my family so live out their purpose in life that they would ultimately be called, "blessed," - a signal showing their journey toward sainthood.

As the baby, John the Baptist leaped in his mother's womb acknowledging the person and presence of Jesus Christ, I pray Holy Mary that my family salutes Christ today in their lives. May they also recognize his presence in the lives of those around them and give honor and praise.

Holy Mary, you were blessed by Elizabeth because you not only believed you would bear a son through the Holy Spirit but that Elizabeth in her old age would bear a son.

May my family believe the word of God. Let God's truth penetrate their minds and hearts resulting in a faith that works in love.

May my family like you, Holy Mary, rejoice in God our Savior and proclaim his greatness today, in word and in action.

Amen.

YOUR RESPONSE TO THE PRAYER YOU PRAY FOR YOUR FAMILY

Yes, Lord. I embrace these prayers I pray today, and I choose to serve others with generosity and love as I magnify your name.

Amen.

3. The Nativity of our Lord Jesus Christ

Now while Mary and Joseph were in Bethlehem,
the time came for her to have her child. And she gave
birth to a son, her firstborn, and laid
him in a manger.

Luke 2

May my family give birth to Jesus today, in their words, their actions in all that they do. May Jesus be born in my families lives - his holiness, his purity, his attentiveness to his mother, his devotion to his father, his hard work as a carpenter, and most of all, his love.

Holy Mary, the shepherds and the wise men came rejoicing. May my families' lives bring others to rejoice as they see Christ born in them.

Protect my family, Holy Mary, from those sources that would seek to harm the presence of Jesus like Herod did, seeking to kill him. There are forces today aligned against your Holy Son and against those who follow him. Sanctify my families' hearts, and may they be ready to give a reason for the hope that is in them, a hope and courage to stand up against those who attack Christ and his message of love and truth.
(See I Peter 3:15).

Holy Mary, may Christ's presence bring joy today in the lives of my family, the joy of having Christ there with them.

May my family be Christ centered and not world centered. May their focus be on Jesus today, and may they be able to say with St. Paul: "My purpose for living is Christ!" (Philippians 1:21)

Amen.

To reinforce this mystery Pray the Our Father, ten Hail Marys, the Glory Be and the Fatima Prayer

YOUR RESPONSE TO THE PRAYER YOU PRAY
FOR YOUR FAMILY

Yes, Lord. I choose to let Christ be born in my life today, to let others see that he is my Lord and Savior and through that bring peace to your world.

Amen.

4. The Presentation of our Lord

Observing the law, they took
Jesus to Jerusalem to present him to the Lord.
Luke 2

It was because of the law of God that you, Holy Mary, brought Jesus to be circumcised and then to present him to God his Father. Pray for my family that they might also walk in obedience to the laws of God, not serving him out of duty only, but out of devotion to God Almighty.

Holy Mary, there were godly people, Simeon and Anna, who prayed for you, Joseph and Jesus. May my family also have holy and godly people who will pray for them. Give them family and friends who will circle them in their prayers and holy encouragement.

Holy Mary, you were told that a sword would pierce your heart. At this time of giving, of sacrifice, of obedience to God, you were informed of the pain that would follow. And you received it without complaining or arguing.

May my family today better understand the pain (physical, emotional, mental) that comes to them, pain that can be redemptive, useful, purifying, preparing them to live with you, Holy Mary, in that eternal heavenly abode.

I pray that my family would grow like Jesus did in wisdom and favor before God and others.

Amen.

YOUR RESPONSE TO THE PRAYER YOU PRAY
FOR YOUR FAMILY

Yes, LORD. I choose to walk in obedience to your laws, knowing that they are there not to restrict me but to release me to live in ways that bring the most glory to you and ultimate pleasure to me.

Amen.

5. Finding Jesus in the Temple

When Jesus was twelve years old, they went to
Jerusalem…and they found him in the Temple sitting
among the doctors listening to them and asking questions.

Luke 2

Holy Mary, may my family exhibit the same wisdom and
understanding Jesus displayed in the Temple before the elders
and teachers. As they walk with people today and interact
with them, give them this special, heavenly wisdom.   May
they long for it, drink it in and embrace it.   Help them that
they might not be tempted to think like the world.

St. Paul said that we as Christians no longer think like the
natural man but the spiritual man because "we have the mind
of Christ." (I Corinthians 2:14-16).

Help my family today, Holy Mary, to draw from that spiritual
gift given at their baptism, the mind of Christ, so that they can
think and speak with wisdom and grace.

Holy Mary, I ask that my family will be given a "hearing
heart" like God gave Solomon, the king of Israel. May they,

like sheep, hear the voice of our shepherd Jesus Christ and follow him in spirit and truth.

At our confirmation, the Holy Spirit was given to each of us and he gave us spiritual gifts that help us live the Christian life. May the seven gifts of the Holy Spirit be evidenced today in my family's life, the spirit of wisdom and understanding, the spirit of counsel and strength, the spirit of knowledge, piety and the fear of the Lord.

Amen.

To reinforce this mystery Pray the Our Father, ten Hail Marys, the Glory Be and the Fatima Prayer, Hail Holy Queen and the Concluding Prayer

YOUR RESPONSE TO THE PRAYER YOU PRAY
FOR YOUR FAMILY

Yes, LORD. I do not want to be known for just knowledge, but wisdom, your wisdom. I choose to live in such a way so that I can be truly wise, full of your Spirit, hearing the voice of Jesus.

Amen.

The
SORROWFUL
Mysteries

II. SORROWFUL MYSTERIES

Tuesday & Friday

On these days we focus on pain, the HOLY PAIN Jesus went through for us. This journey takes Jesus into a realm that we all tend to avoid. We hate pain. We run from suffering. We abhor death. We want life to be easy, comfortable and serene. Yet we know that if we never face battles, there will be no victories. As they say: "no pain, no gain."

Too often we ask: "Why am I suffering since God is all loving and powerful and can stop my pain in an instant?" The answer is simple. God will often not stop our suffering because HE DIDN'T STOP HIS SUFFERING. He knows that suffering and pain on his and our part can be redemptive and bring about eternal and glorious changes both to us and to others. This is why praying the Sorrowful Mysteries is so important.

These mysteries take us progressively to the cross, a place that is foundational to our theology. It is here that love and suffering meet, and something deeply profound occurs - the redemption of humankind. This is where we enter into the Holy of Holies, a place where the lamb was taken with its blood sprinkled on the altar - for us. What a holy moment! God dying for us - love conquering our sin.

As we move through these Sorrowful Mysteries, we must, as it were, take off our shoes, for we are on holy ground. Never has such a thing been done - the creator dying for the creature, the pure dying for the impure, the King dying for his servants. It is unthinkable, a mystery that can never be fully solved, so deep it is, so surprising, so awesome in all its nuances.

This dark time in the history of humankind is the brightest point of all.

Oh how he loves you and me!

Though it is Jesus our Savior dying, we are called to be with him, to unite ourselves with his suffering and thus be a redemptive force to our families, friends and all people in our world. It is when we join ourselves to Christ's suffering that we can ultimately move toward the resurrected life, a life that is full of power, glory and joy.

Let us suffer WITH Christ as we move with him through these Sorrowful Mysteries. Let us experience his pain, his loneliness, his rejection and his death as he joyfully endured the cross.

It would be great if you were willing to suffer for your family. There are times you may fast or do other penances with them in mind so that God will see your sacrifice and use that to be redemptive in their lives.

1. The Agony of Jesus in the Garden

Jesus came to Gethsemane. And sadness came over him,
and great distress. He knelt and prayed,
"Father if you are willing, take this cup from me, but not
my will but yours be done." Luke 22

Holy Mary, your son was not afraid to struggle in the garden, to face loneliness, pain and death.   May Jesus your son grant my family the grace to struggle, to face sorrow, to feel distress and not run and hide from the difficulties in life.

Holy Mary, teach my family to pray like Jesus prayed as he faced the horror of death on the cross and bearing the sins of the world. Help my family to run to you for aid, for hope and for consolation.

We all want to run from pain and suffering, Holy Mary. We want to have life OUR way and not HIS WAY, a way that includes suffering and pain. May my family be able to say with all their heart:

Not my will BUT THINE BE DONE.

May my family realize that the life that Christ leads them on is not one where there is an absence of pain and anxiety but rather an absence of interior discord that results in a supernatural peace even during the storms of life.

Holy Mary, pray for my family that they might be saved from self centeredness, living for themselves alone. Make them like John the Baptist who sought to decrease that Christ might increase. Reduce me and my family to love, an all encompassing charity that gives all of ourselves to God and others, that I and they might find true life, life to the full.

Amen.

To reinforce this mystery Pray the Our Father, ten Hail Marys,
the Glory Be and the Fatima Prayer

YOUR RESPONSE TO THE PRAYER YOU PRAY
FOR YOUR FAMILY

Yes, LORD. I admit that I want to have it MY WAY. I confess how hard it is to submit to YOUR WAY, to put aside my will, my plans, my wishes, my hopes and dreams and allow YOU to develop your hopes and dreams in me and for me. I know that in the end, YOUR WAY is the ONLY WAY that leads to true happiness and joy. So...I submit, freely, fully, willfully my life into your hands.

> Have thine own way Lord
> Have thine own way
> Thou art the potter
> I am the clay
> Mold me and make me
> After thy will
> While I am waiting
> Yielded and still.
> Amen.

Adelaide A. Pollard, author 1906

2. The Scourging at the Pillar

And they bound Jesus and handed him over to
Pilate. Pilate then had Jesus taken away and scourged.

Luke 23

Holy Mary, pray to Jesus for my family that they, like him, may learn how to face rejection and injustice. Barabbas, who should have been scourged and crucified, was let go and the innocent man, Jesus, was scourged and crucified. Help my family to bear injustice willingly when they face rebuke and punishment, instead of the success and praise they may deserve. Give them joy, knowing that they can suffer with and for Jesus in this way.

Help them, Holy Mary, to face each blow in life, each painful moment with joy, knowing that it can be a redemptive force for others (see Col. 1:24).

May they be willing to be mocked for their faith, fully bowing to the whip of angry, demeaning and resentful words.

May they be able to say: "Forgive them, dear Jesus, for they do not know what they do."

Amen.

To reinforce this mystery Pray the Our Father, ten Hail Marys, the Glory Be and the Fatima Prayer

YOUR RESPONSE TO THE PRAYER YOU PRAY
FOR YOUR FAMILY

Yes, LORD. I know that too often life is not fair. Yet in the end, your justice will make everything right. Thank you that, as King of the Universe, your wise judgments will one day win over all that is wrong. Today, I trust and rest in your loving justice.

Amen.

3. Jesus is Crowned with Thorns

They stripped him and dressed him up in purple.

And having twisted some thorns into a crown,

they put this on his head.

Matthew 27

Holy Mother of God, we all desire to be crowned with honor and receive the recognition we feel we deserve. We want to be accepted, affirmed and appreciated.   Teach my family today, that when they are willing to stand up for their faith, to face ridicule and rejection because of their belief in Jesus, when they are crowned with disgust and disapproval, that their ultimate crown of glory will be in heaven.   May my family be willing to wait…that they might win!

Holy Mother of God, it seems that the mockery of your son would never come to an end. On and on the soldiers laughed at him, whipped him, stripped him of all honor and glory…at least on the outside. But he stood firm, with a glory and honor none could ever take away. For this mockery made him an even greater hero, OUR HERO, our savior, our Lord.

Teach my family, Holy Mother, how to endure like Jesus did, in the face of what may seem full defeat, to find honor and glory in their suffering, to see it as a crown of glory instead of a crown of shame.

May my family learn the glorious lessons of suffering today, Holy Mary, my Mother, our Mother who patiently endured the torture of your holy son.

Amen.

To reinforce this mystery Pray the Our Father, ten Hail Marys, the Glory Be and the Fatima Prayer

YOUR RESPONSE TO THE PRAYER YOU PRAY FOR YOUR FAMILY

Yes, LORD. I admit I love to be honored, affirmed and appreciated for what I have done. Teach me to be willing to receive the thorny crowns of condemnation, rejection and ridicule, if it is given because I fully follow you. Give me the strength to endure.

Amen.

4. Jesus Carried the Cross

And he carried his own cross as they
led him out to crucify him.
Then they seized a man, Simon of Cyrene and
made him shoulder the cross and carry it behind Jesus.

John 19

Holy Mary, what crosses does my family have to carry today? What pain must they bear?   What rejection, what physical, emotional, mental suffering must they endure?   Holy Mary Mother of God, let my family not run from their crosses but bear them with the endurance aided by the Holy Spirit.

Today the world wants us to get all we can, to avoid pain at any cost, to run from our problems, sickness and hardships, to leave a struggling marriage and give in to temptations that will destroy us. Holy Mary, may my family be willing to face each difficult situation and find strength to carry the cross even as Jesus found strength.

Give my family someone who will stand with them, to help them bear their crosses. May my family also be willing to help others, today, to bear their crosses.

Holy Mary, when a member of my family falls, runs out of strength and wants to give up, give them hope and courage to keep going. If someone in my family needs special courage today, may Jesus stand with them and give them hope. Let my family see that "your grace is sufficient" for any trial they may face, any cross they have to bear.

Amen.

To reinforce this mystery Pray the Our Father, ten Hail Marys,
the Glory Be and the Fatima Prayer

YOUR RESPONSE TO THE PRAYER YOU PRAY FOR YOUR FAMILY

Yes, LORD. Carrying my crosses causes a weariness that, at times, makes me want to quit. Yet I haven't! That's because of your support and strength as well as the help of others praying for me and encouraging me. Help me to encourage others who have crosses to bear, sickness, hardships, difficulties that seek to destroy them. May I be that help that gets them across the finish line…to you.

Amen.

5. The Crucifixion of our Lord

They crucified him. Luke 23

Holy Mary, my family doesn't want to die. They will do everything to avoid the cross. But if my family is going to find life, they must die to themselves that they might live forever.

My family is "crucified with Christ," so that they might live a new life with power to overcome any test or temptation. Holy Mary, let my family identify themselves with the crucified Christ and embrace his redemptive death.

Help my family to embrace the cross today. May they make the sign of the cross over their body and claim its redemptive power. May we all, family and friends, be a family of the cross.

Holy Mary, help me and my family to be willing to die for others, today, to die to our own desires and to live for others.

May we be redemptive, reconciling forces in our world.

Amen.

To reinforce this mystery Pray the Our Father, ten Hail Marys,
the Glory Be and the Fatima Prayer, Hail Holy Queen and the
Concluding Prayer

YOUR RESPONSE TO THE PRAYER YOU PRAY FOR YOUR FAMILY

Yes, LORD. I don't want to die. But if I am going to live with you forever, I MUST DIE to self and my own way. If I do this, I will find true life, life that is full and overflowing with joy. So…I choose to die with Christ that I might live in abundance now and forever.

Amen.

The GLORIOUS Mysteries

III. GLORIOUS MYSTERIES

Wednesday & Sunday

Glory. Victory. This is what we all want. All of life is moving towards this glorious end, and all who are in Christ will experience it…forever!

Each of these mysteries is called a mystery because we don't fully understand it nor can we drink in all it means. None of us has seen a resurrection or an ascension. The Holy Spirit is something that is hard to get our minds around. We can picture God the Father as an old man with a beard and Jesus Christ with his smile and love written in his eyes. But the Holy Spirit, this third member of the Trinity, is a little foggy in our minds. Yet, what a difference he makes when he comes into our lives, brings a pile of gifts and gives us the power to live our Catholic Faith.

Last, there is the focus on our Blessed Mother. What a MOM!

You know, don't you, that she was made our mother at the cross when Jesus turned to the apostle John and said, "Behold your mother," and to his mother Mary, "Behold your son?"

The early church taught that Jesus was making Mary the mother of us all since John was an apostle, a foundation and leader of the early church. And beyond Mary being officially named as the Mother of the Church at the cross, Mary did give birth to the God-man Jesus who founded the church. Thus, this giving birth makes her not only the mother of the God-man, Jesus, but also the mother of the church, birthing the church from her holy womb, a miracle of God's grace.

Ah! What grace!

It was quite an extraordinary journey Mary took to bring the redeemer to us, birthing him, watching his ministry and then to stand at the cross and see him die. Then what joy was hers to welcome her resurrected son - what a reunion that was, her holy son, redeemer of the world!

We see her FULL of grace - overflowing with no room for sin - not a speck. Her sinless character only came about not on her own merit but through the grace of God her father, saving her from original sin in her mother's womb (a truth taught by the early church and even some early Protestant leaders). Because of this, her son Jesus could not let her be chained to the grave when she was so pure and holy.

There was and is none like her.

So these glorious mysteries end with her in heaven, reigning as QUEEN, serving a powerful role for us. It is also a prefiguring of us as we too, if we are faithful, will as St. Paul says, "reign" with Christ (Romans 5:17).

1. The Resurrection of Jesus Christ

He is risen from the dead.

Come and see the place where he lay. Matthew 28

Holy Mary, Jesus destroyed death that we might live. May my family be so connected with Jesus; through their faith, through their baptism, through their regular taking of the Eucharist and through their holy and loving actions, that they too might enjoy this resurrection.

Give my family today, the HOPE of the resurrection deep in their heart. May they long for it, embrace it, and cherish this coming event for all the baptized who continue to live out this baptism.

> *Life is short.*
> *Death is sure.*
> *Sin the cause.*
> *Christ the cure.*

May my family, Holy Mary, truly believe in Christ Jesus the Lord and not fix their hope on this world but on Jesus and the world to come.

Holy Mary, may the resurrected Christ live in their hearts, giving them supernatural power, resurrection power to live their lives each day.

Thank you, Holy Mary, that your son is alive and his life gives us hope that we too will live forever. May my family live under the shadow of this hope.

Amen.

To reinforce this mystery Pray the Our Father, ten Hail Marys,
the Glory Be and the Fatima Prayer

YOUR RESPONSE TO THE PRAYER YOU PRAY FOR YOUR FAMILY

Yes, LORD. I choose to allow this resurrected Christ to live in me and have hope that I too will be resurrected to eternal life.

Amen.

2. The Ascension of Jesus to Heaven

The Lord Jesus was taken up into heaven and took his
seat at the right hand of God. Mark 16

Holy Mary, your son is seated at the right hand of the Father,
a place of honor and power. There he lives to pray for us.

Pray for my family Holy Jesus that they would experience
your full salvation. And Holy Mary, join with me in this
prayer to Jesus that all my friends and family might, today,
join with you in love and devotion to your son.

Holy Mary, your son left earth but did not leave us alone. He
sent the Holy Spirit to be with us, and with the Holy Spirit
Jesus abides in us.

May the presence of your son be felt today by my family.
Come Holy Jesus, come Holy Spirit, come Holy Father and
protect my family on their journey, that one day they too will
be joined to Jesus, reigning in heaven forever and ever.

Holy Mary, when your son left he gave us work to do until he
comes again. May my family be faithful in accomplishing

those holy tasks by loving God, loving others and living out their faith.

Amen.

YOUR RESPONSE TO THE PRAYER YOU PRAY
FOR YOUR FAMILY

Yes, LORD. Thanks for being in heaven praying for me. Without you I can do nothing. But with you, I can do anything.

Amen.

3. THE DECENT OF THE HOLY SPIRIT

When Pentecost came, they were all filled
with the Holy Spirit. Acts 2

Holy Mary, may my family never feel alone and abandoned by God.   Help them to embrace the presence of the Holy Spirit and the JOY he brings.

As the Holy Spirit lives in my family, may they experience the fullness of his gifts, Holy Mary.   May the 7 gifts of the Holy Spirit be evidenced today in each of my families lives:

- *the spirit of wisdom*
- *and understanding,*
- *the spirit of counsel*
- *and strength,*
- *the spirit of knowledge,*
- *piety and*
- *the fear of the Lord.*

Isaiah 11: 2-3

Release in my family, Lord Jesus, the **FRUIT** of the Holy Spirit mentioned in Galatians 5:22.

Love - Joy - Peace - Patience - Kindness - Generosity
Faithfulness - Gentleness - Self Control

May my family develop the **7 VIRTUES** powered by the Holy Spirit, in contrast to the 7 deadly sins.

1. **Temperance** - as opposed to *Gluttony*

2. **Patience** - as opposed to *Anger and Wrath*

3. **Kindness** - as opposed to *Envy*

4. **Humility** - as opposed to *Pride*

5. **Diligence** - as opposed to *Sloth and Spiritual laziness*

6. **Chastity** - as opposed to *Lust*

7. **Charity** - as opposed to *Greed*

Amen.

To reinforce this mystery Pray the Our Father, ten Hail Marys,
the Glory Be and the Fatima Prayer

YOUR RESPONSE TO THE PRAYER YOU PRAY
FOR YOUR FAMILY

Yes, LORD. I need the Holy Spirit today. May his gifts, fruit and virtues permeate my life.

Amen.

4. The Assumption of Mary into Heaven

Come then my love, my lovely one, come. Song 2

Hail Mary, FULL OF GRACE. Luke 2

Holy Mary, your body did not see corruption, but you were brought by your son to heaven to be with him and to pray for us. Thank you for your faithfulness in praying for my family. I am grateful that, though millions pray to you, you hear each one of us and bring those requests to Jesus your son. Pray for us now, Holy Mary, for my entire family, that we might receive the full promises of Christ and enter into his heavenly abode so that we might be with him and you forever.

What a powerful woman you are, Holy Mary. What a holy position you have in heaven. Because of this, I pray to you for your constant intercession for my family. Pray for them now. You know their needs. Bring them to Jesus.

Holy Mary, you are pure and perfect in all your ways and were protected from sin in your mother's womb by the grace of God who overshadowed you so that you could be a clean and pure vessel for your holy son. Your assumption gives us hope of our being caught up to be with Jesus forever.

Prepare my family today that they might be made worthy to be in the presence of your son and our redeemer.

Amen.

YOUR RESPONSE TO THE PRAYER YOU PRAY FOR YOUR FAMILY

Yes, LORD. Bring me to yourself as you brought to yourself your Holy Mother. May I one day be accepted into your presence where I can live with you, your Mother and the entire family of God forever and ever.

Amen.

5. Mary is Crowned as Queen of Heaven and Earth

A great sign appeared in the sky, a woman clothed with the sun, with the moon under her feet. Revelation 12

Holy Mary, the early Church and Fathers agree that you were crowned with glory as Queen of heaven and earth. May my family also receive their crown, a "crown of righteousness" promised "to all who have longed for his (Jesus Christ) appearance" (see II Timothy 4:8).

Holy Mary, your son took the blows that he may now take the bows, as "every knee shall bow and every tongue in heaven and earth proclaim him to be Lord' (Philippians 2: 9-11). Your son's exaltation came because of his great humility and service.

You too, Holy Mother, were humble, giving birth to the king of the universe in a lowly manger. You watched as Satan tried to kill him. And then you gently encouraged him to accomplish his first miracle of turning water into wine because you knew who he was. Yet you held, closely in your heart, this great secret until it was time to share it with the world.

Now, because of your great humility and gentle quietness, always focused on your son and never on yourself, you have been exalted like he, and crowned with glory. May my family learn this gentleness of yours, this quiet humility, that they too will one day in glory, receive their crown, because they were faithful to the calling of pointing people to your son, Jesus.

Holy Mary, Queen of heaven and earth, I acknowledge what holiness and honor has been given to you. May my family live lives worthy that they too may receive this holiness and honor.

Amen.

To reinforce this mystery Pray the Our Father, ten Hail Marys, the Glory Be and the Fatima Prayer, Hail Holy Queen and the Concluding Prayer

YOUR RESPONSE TO THE PRAYER YOU PRAY FOR YOUR FAMILY

Yes, LORD. I have too often tried to be king or queen of my own realm and thus lacked the humility Blessed Mary had, a humility that helped to lift her to her high position in heaven. Today, I choose to walk humbly before you and others, that I too might win the prize - a crown of righteousness and eternal life.

Amen.

The
LUMINOUS
Mysteries

IV. LUMINOUS MYSTERIES

Thursday

John's gospel states that: "the light came into the world but people preferred darkness to the light." Then he goes on to say: "But everyone who loves the truth COMES TO THE LIGHT."

Again in John's first epistle he writes: "If we walk in the light as he (Jesus) is in the light, we have fellowship with one another and the blood of Jesus cleanses us from all sin."

It was St. Paul who said in his letter to the Ephesians: "You were once darkness, but now you are light in the Lord. Live as children of the light, for light produces every kind of goodness and righteousness and truth."

This is why we pray the Luminous Mysteries, that we might focus on Jesus the light, and then, because he lives in us, to let that light shine in us, to our families and then on to the world.

Jesus proclaimed: "You are the light of the world." Let us fully live this out as we walk in the light of his presence, that presence where our Blessed Mother is, who is also in the light praying that we would be messengers of her son who "enlightens every person who comes into the world."

1. The Baptism in the Jordan

And Jesus was baptized by John, and suddenly the
heavens opened. Matthew 3

Holy Mary, in your son's baptism he prefigured his death and resurrection as he entered into the water (death) and came out (resurrection). May my family be so identified with Christ today, that they might be dead to sin and alive in your son.

It was at your son's baptism that the Holy Spirit came and declared him to be the son of the Father. Holy Mary, may my family experience the assurance that they are members of God's family, that God loves them and lives in them by means of the Holy Spirit.

Holy Mary, as my family goes to Mass and dips their finger into the water upon entry, may they renew their baptismal vows to live faithfully, wholly devoted to you as their Mother and to your son, Jesus Christ.

For those in my family who have not experienced the Sacrament of Baptism, pray for them, Holy Mother, that they would be baptized and thus find forgiveness of sins, the fullness of the Holy Spirit, and become part of the body of your son, Jesus Christ.

Amen.

To reinforce this mystery Pray the Our Father, ten Hail Marys,
the Glory Be and the Fatima Prayer

YOUR RESPONSE TO THE PRAYER YOU PRAY FOR YOUR FAMILY

Yes, LORD. Help me by your Spirit to live out my baptism, dead to the world and all it offers and alive to you, my Lord and my God.

Amen.

2. The Wedding at Cana

There was a wedding at Cana, and the Mother of
Jesus was there. Jesus and his disciples had
also been invited. John 2

Holy Mary, your son blessed a marriage by his presence and through his first miracle. I pray that you would ask Jesus to be present in my families' marriages (if married) and bring joy to their marriages.

Holy Mary, your son took what was ordinary and made it extraordinary - water into wine. Pray to your son that he would do that for my marriage as well as all the marriages of my family. May we experience the new wine, the freshness, the surprises that only Jesus can bring. And if not married, take the new wine of your Spirit and bring refreshment, fulfillment and joy to their lives.

The Sacrament of Marriage is vitally important in our day when marriage and family is being attacked. Holy Mary, as with any Sacrament, may supernatural grace be released so that this natural relationship becomes supernaturally lived.

I pray, Holy Mary, that the Holy Spirit will inhabit my marriage and the marriages of our family members and friends in such a way that each married person will demonstrate the sacrificial love manifested by your son, Jesus Christ. May we realize that all irritations, difficulties and hardships work to shape us to be more like Jesus. Help us to be willing to die for each other so that we might, in the end, live joyously together.

Amen

To reinforce this mystery Pray the Our Father, ten Hail Marys,
the Glory Be and the Fatima Prayer

YOUR RESPONSE TO THE PRAYER YOU PRAY
FOR YOUR FAMILY

Yes, LORD. Take the wine of your grace Lord Jesus, and bless my marriage. And whether married or not married, lead me to where YOU, Lord, might be the center, sustainer and bringer of joy in my life.

Amen.

3. The Proclamation of the Kingdom

The time has come. The kingdom of God is close at hand.
Repent and believe the Good News. Mark 1

Holy Mary, so that I and my family may be fully welcomed into God's eternal kingdom, pray to Jesus that each of us might repent of our sins, be born of water and Spirit, accept Jesus like a little child, and be "poor in spirit" that we might be rich in the Kingdom of God.

May this prayer of the publican written below be on my family's lips today…

**Jesus Christ, Son of God, have
mercy on me a sinner.**

May my family learn how to love their enemies, Holy Mary. When we were still enemies of Christ, because of our sin, he nevertheless loved us. Holy Mary, pray that my family would be given this kind of supernatural love for others, even their enemies, a love that is necessary to enter into the Kingdom of God.

Bring my family into the Church of your son, the One, Holy, Catholic and Apostolic Church, which is an expression of Christ's Kingdom on earth.

Holy Mary, may my family constantly avail themselves of the Sacrament of Reconciliation, the repentance of sin and the forgiveness that follows so that my family might live a holy life with your son in his Kingdom forever.

Amen

To reinforce this mystery Pray the Our Father, ten Hail Marys, the Glory Be and the Fatima Prayer

YOUR RESPONSE TO THE PRAYER YOU PRAY
FOR YOUR FAMILY

Yes, LORD. May I seek first the KINGDOM OF GOD and his righteousness so that I may enter fully into your kingdom.

Amen.

4. The Transfiguration

As Jesus prayed, he was transfigured.
His face shone like the sun and his clothes became as
dashing as light. Luke 9

Holy Mary, the glory of God leaked through your son in such a magnificent way! Pray that this glory, in some small way, may be exhibited in my life and the life of my family. May people see that God is in us. I pray that this manifestation would not be in word only, but in a display of his supernatural glory - the glory of his holiness, the glory of his truth, the glory of his love.

Lift any darkness; depression, fear, anxiety and any sin that blocks the light of Christ and dooms any member of my family to defeat.

SHINE JESUS SHINE!

I pray, Holy Mary, that my family would see that Jesus is the focus and center of our Church and that nothing should take the place of him. Save us from being caught up on side issues that would take away our focus and attention on Jesus.

May I and each family member learn how to "listen to HIM," to your son, Holy Mary. Give us ears to hear his voice, the voice of the shepherd and to know his ways as we live our lives on earth.

As Jesus took his disciples up to a mountain to pray, ask Jesus, Holy Mary, to teach me and my family how to pray, to spend time with God our Father, to be away from the crowds and to be quiet before him.

Amen

To reinforce this mystery Pray the Our Father, ten Hail Marys, the Glory Be and the Fatima Prayer

YOUR RESPONSE TO THE PRAYER YOU PRAY FOR YOUR FAMILY

Yes, LORD. I choose to spend time in the light, to walk with the Light, Jesus Christ my Lord. Keep me from distractions that would take my focus off the centrality of all that is… Jesus Christ, the Light of the world.

Amen.

5. The Institution of the Eucharist

I am the living bread that comes down from heaven.
Whoever EATS MY FLESH AND DRINKS MY BLOOD
lives in me and I in him.   John 6

This is MY BODY given for you. Matthew 26

Holy Mother, may my family regularly receive the Eucharist, the bread and wine transformed into the body, blood, soul and divinity of Jesus Christ your son.   May my family acknowledge your son's presence in the bread and wine, and may they find life and hope as they receive your son's life given for them.

Thank you, Holy Mary, that your son brings our family and friends closer together. For as we take the Eucharist, we not only have physical bonds that tie us to each other, but we become a spiritual family, brothers and sisters of your son, Jesus Christ. May we see this, revel in it and walk in the light of this awesome relationship.

Holy Mary, as your son gave his all for us, may my family give their all for others. Pray that my family would be saved from selfishness. May they learn the value of sacrifice and what it means to give themselves fully for others.

Amen

To reinforce this mystery Pray the Our Father, ten Hail Marys, the Glory Be and the Fatima Prayer, Hail Holy Queen and the Concluding Prayer

YOUR RESPONSE TO THE PRAYER YOU PRAY
FOR YOUR FAMILY

Yes, LORD. What a gift, the Eucharist, true food for the soul! I choose to receive it often and to spread the word about the food that brings eternal life, Jesus Christ, the true manna.

Amen.

Now that you have read the prayers that you pray for YOUR FAMILY why not begin to use my other book…

I'm Praying The ROSARY for YOU!

This could greatly impact your family members in ways that you will never know until you get to heaven.

Order some copies and **send that book to every family member as well as some friends**. The cost of this will be far outweighed by the eternal dividends it will reap.

This ROSARY book will be **personalized** especially for them with their **names written in all the prayers**. In so doing you will be a *source of encouragement* as they see that you are praying regularly for them.

MOST PEOPLE HAVE NO ONE TO PRAY FOR THEM!

Change the tide. Make sure that every one within your circle of family and friends are being prayed for... AND THEY KNOW IT!

START THIS REVOLUTION OF PRAYER

TODAY!

Outline of your prayer
for YOUR FAMILY

1. I make the sign of the cross
2. I say the Apostles Creed
3. I pray the OUR FATHER
4. I say the Hail Mary
5. I pray the Gloria Be
6. I pray the Fatima Prayer
7. I end each Rosary (after praying the 5 Mysteries) with the Hail Holy Queen and the Concluding Prayer

1. The **JOYFUL** Mysteries (Mon/Sat)

1) The Annunciation
2) The Visitation
3) The Nativity
4) The Presentation
5) Finding Jesus in the Temple

2. The **SORROWFUL** Mysteries (Tues/Fri)

1) Agony in the garden
2) Scourging at the pillar
3) Crowning with thorns
4) Carrying the cross
5) Crucifixion

3. The **GLORIOUS** Mysteries (Wed/Sun)

1) The Resurrection

2) The Ascension

3) Descent of the Holy Spirit

4) Assumption of Mary

5) Coronation of Mary

4. The **LUMINOUS** Mysteries (Thurs)

1) Baptism of Jesus - *Sacrament of Baptism*

2) Feast at Cana - *Sacrament of Marriage*

3) Preaching the Kingdom - *Sacrament of Reconciliation, Sacrament of Last Rites and Healing of the sick*

4) The Transfiguration - *Sacrament of Confirmation and Sacrament of Holy Orders*

5) The Eucharist - *The Blessed Sacrament*

8. All the while I ask the Holy Spirit to give me insight so that I can pray specifically for each member of my family as I pray the Rosary.

Amen!

Now…
May God use your prayer
for your family
and draw them closer
to the God who loves them
and wants the best for THEM!

Amen.

Your closing prayer for YOUR FAMILY

May God give my family courage
To be all THEY were meant to be
To allow the God who made THEM
To INVADE every area of their lives
Their...Soul
Their...Personality
Their...Social life
Their...Physical and Mental life
Their...Spiritual life
Changing it, infusing it with himself
Today
Tomorrow
Until they die
For the glory of Christ
Amen

Spread the word!

Phone, text, email or tell friends at
Facebook, Instagram, etc.
Make it a goal to communicate
with *AT LEAST 10 OTHERS*
who will greatly benefit from using this book.
Tell them how it could change their lives and the lives of
others.
Don't keep quiet.

Spread the news

Change…a person
Change…a family
Change…the world!

Questions about Mary
Mother of Jesus Christ

1. Did Mary have other children besides Jesus? The Bible talks about Jesus's brothers and sisters. Doesn't this counter the teaching of the Catholic Church?

The Catholic Church as well as some other well known Protestants teach that Mary was ALWAYS a virgin. Note these statements from famous Protestant leaders.

Martin Luther, the main leader of the Protestant Reformation wrote:

> *When Matthew says that Joseph did not know Mary carnally until she had brought forth her son, it does not follow that he knew her subsequently; on the contrary, it means that he never did know her.*

> *Christ, our Savior, was the real and natural fruit of Mary's virginal womb. This was without the cooperation of a man, and she remained a virgin after*

*that. Christ was the only Son of Mary, and **the Virgin Mary bore no children besides Him**. I am inclined to agree with those who declare that 'brothers' really mean 'cousins' here, for Holy Writ and the Jews always call cousins brothers.* (Sermons on John)

Zwingli, an early Protestant leader wrote:

*I firmly believe that Mary, according to the words of the gospel as a pure Virgin brought forth for us the Son of God in childbirth and **after childbirth forever remained a pure, intact Virgin**.* (Zwingli Opera, Corpus Reformatorum, Berlin, 1905, v. 1, p. 424)

Even **John Wesley**, founder of the Methodists wrote in 1749:

*I believe that He [Jesus] was made man, joining the human nature with the divine in one person; being conceived by the singular operation of the Holy Ghost, and born of the blessed Virgin Mary, who, as well after as before she brought Him forth, **continued a pure and unspotted virgin**.* (a letter written to the Roman Catholic Church)

2. Why pray to Mary since there is "Only one mediator between God and man, the man Christ Jesus," as stated by St. Paul to Timothy?

It is true that Jesus Christ paid for our sins and in this way is our own personal Savior and redeemer. Mary is not a redeemer in the same way Christ is. Yet she can intercede and mediate for us in her own unique way. Even as I ask someone to pray for me, to intercede and mediate (as a priest does - for we are all made priests in Christ), so too I can ask Mary to intercede and mediate for me. This in no way takes away from the redemptive and salvific redemptive action on Christ's part. It is he who shed his blood for the redemption of all humankind.

It is interesting, as we look deeper into this question, that Catholics and Protestants approach prayer differently. Catholics see all those in the family of God, whether those who have gone on to eternal life or those still alive on the earth as a GREAT AND GRAND GROUP as a whole, all working together to bring about the Kingdom of God. ALL of them are engaged in this activity. So, as a Catholic prays to Jesus, he also asks the whole company of saints to pray with him, including the Holy Mother of God, Mary.

Other Christians tend to ignore this great company, this great army fighting to bring in the kingdom of God. Why exclude them? Why not allow them to fight for you and to pray with you?

3. Do Catholics worship Mary?

Absolutely not! We worship only the Father, Son and the Holy Spirit. Mary is not part of the Trinity! To think so is heresy. Yet we do hold her in high honor even as we do some of the greats of history like George Washington, Abraham Lincoln as well as St. Mother Teresa and so many others.

Mary, the Blessed Mother of Jesus Christ, can even be held in a higher honor only because of her special favor, to be the vessel that gave birth to the King of the Universe, God in the flesh! What honor! Therefore it is right and good that we should honor her too in a very special way.

4. How can Mary hear all our prayers since millions are praying to her at the same time?

Do you understand time? If a million people wanted to speak to you, you would have to take TIME to hear each one. And if you gave each of them a minute of your time, it would take a million minutes to hear each one which is nearly 17,000 hours or approximately two years!

BUT THERE IS NO TIME IN HEAVEN. When you move into that spiritual universe, many of the limits we have here are removed. Thus what is impossible here is possible there so that Mary can hear us all, even when millions pray through her to Jesus.

5. It says in the Bible that "ALL have sinned and come short of God's glory." How is it then that Mary is said to not have sinned. Isn't this a direct contradiction of the Scriptures? Doesn't Mary call God her Savior?

It is true that Mary needed a Savior. This is why she calls God her Savior. Yet you need to understand what she means. Our Holy Mother was SAVED from original sin BY GOD'S GRACE. On her own, Mary would have been a sinner just like you and me. But, because of God's special plan to make her into a perfect vessel for his Son, Jesus Christ, he stepped in and did something unique, he SAVED HER from sin by preventing her from any participation in it. And even as the man Jesus was protected from sin through the working of the Holy Spirit, so too, Mary was saved from sin, and by the power of the Holy Spirit lived a perfect life.

Yes, all have sinned except for Jesus and Mary, Jesus because he is the Holy Son of God and Mary, because she was to be the holy vessel for the incarnation PROTECTED BY GOD'S GRACE.

Mary, Mary, Quite Contrary

Years ago I stepped into the home of Ernie Harwell, hall of fame announcer for the Detroit Tigers. As I walked into his home, he introduced me to his mother and then left to make a call. I sat there for a moment, making small talk, all the while thinking that I had come to see Ernie, not his mother.

Then it occurred to me that if I wanted to know Ernie better, I needed to take advantage of this time with his mother. So I began to ask her questions about her son and what he was like growing up. In the space of nearly ten minutes, I gleaned some valuable insight to this friend of mine, information that made me appreciate him even more.

At the time I was a Protestant Evangelical pastor with a driving focus in my life - getting to know Jesus and helping others do the same.

Thirty years later, God clearly indicated that I should become a Catholic. There was, however, a major problem, Jesus' mother. I wanted my focus to be on Jesus and not clouded by those who surrounded him, including his mother. I believed she was a good, even a great person. But that was about it. I wanted to spend time with Jesus, my friend and master, not with his mother.

Yet the more I began to look at Mary and pay attention to her, the more I liked this unusual woman. I discovered that she was always putting the focus on Jesus. In fact, that was her purpose in life, to point people to her son. After all, didn't Mary know Jesus better than any other person?

She helped him take his first steps, knew where he was ticklish, what his favorite foods were, and that he always got up early to pray, prayers that sometimes she could hear - their intimacy, openness and power. Mary also saw her son's love for the Hebrew Scriptures which he memorized as an early child. She observed his complete obedience to his heavenly father.

Yet in all of this, Mary never bragged about the intimate details of her son like other women did as they boasted about their children's accomplishments. There was no, "My Son's on the Honor Roll," plastered on the back of her cart. Nor did she write an op ed piece for the Jerusalem Times, talking about all his miracles and how great "MY" son is.

She was amazingly quiet. It was never about her parenting skills and all she did. It was instead all about her Son, Jesus. He was her focus, her life.

Before becoming Catholic, that was my focus too. And now, I find that spending time with Mary pays off with big dividends. She always does what she does best, help me to more fully understand her son.

Thank you, my dear Mother, for always pointing me to Jesus. I was the one that was contrary, not you.

When You Are Short Of Time

Sometimes, hopefully rarely, you don't have time to pray a full Rosary for your family. Yet, even when this happens, you can still pray for them prayers that grab the attention of Mary and Jesus Christ her son.

Use this simple outline
to pray
this shortened version.

1. The **JOYFUL** Mysteries (Mon/Sat)

Begin: *Hail Mary Full Of Grace*
Our Father

1) **The Annunciation:** *Fill them with your GRACE and may they be aware of the presence of God.*

2) **The Visitation:** *Give them a servant's heart like Mary who served Elizabeth. May they, like John the Baptist, salute Jesus Christ today.*

3) **The Nativity:** *May they give birth to Jesus today so that people may see him and find true joy and peace as they glorify God.*

4) **The Presentation:** *May they fully follow God's law with full devotion to him.*

5) **Finding Jesus in the Temple:** *Give them wisdom and spiritual insight today, the mind of Christ that they may think his thoughts and speak his words.*

Close your prayers with
Our Father, Hail Mary, Glory Be, Save them from the fires of hell. Amen.

2. The **SORROWFUL** Mysteries (Tues/Fri)

Begin: *Hail Mary Full Of Grace*
　　　 Our Father

1) **Agony in the garden:** Give them the grace to say: "Not my will but thine be done."

2) **Scourging at the pillar:** *Help them to face rejection and injustice with a forgiving spirit.*

3) **Crowning with thorns:** *May they strive not for earthly crowns and recognition, but for your favor alone.*

4) **Carrying the cross:** *Give them special grace today to bear up under the pain and stress they may feel. And may they lovingly help others carry their crosses.*

5) **Crucifixion:** *Help them to die to self and live for God and others.*

Close your prayers with
　　　 Our Father, Hail Mary, Glory Be, Save them from the fires of hell. Amen.

3. The **GLORIOUS** Mysteries (Wed/Sun)

Begin: *Hail Mary Full Of Grace*
      Our Father

1) The Resurrection: *May they experience the resurrection of eternal life with you, LORD.*

2) The Ascension: *May they know, Jesus, that you are praying for them right now!*

3) Descent of the Holy Spirit: *Come Holy Spirit and release your gifts, fruit and virtues in their lives.*

4) Assumption of Mary: *Holy Mary, may they be brought up to heaven to be with you and your son.*

5) Coronation of Mary: *May they reign with you, Holy Mother, and with your son, forever.*

Close your prayers with
      Our Father, Hail Mary, Glory Be, Save them from the fires of hell. Amen.

4. The **LUMINOUS** Mysteries (Thurs)

Begin: ***Hail Mary Full Of Grace***
      Our Father

1) Baptism of Jesus: *May they live out their baptism, that special connection to you, Lord Jesus.*

2) Feast at Cana: *Give them the spiritual wine of the presence and power of Jesus, releasing joy.*

3) Preaching the Kingdom: *May they repent of sin and find full forgiveness.*

4) The Transfiguration: *Shine Jesus shine in their lives filling them with your power and presence.*

5) The Eucharist: *May they eat regularly your holy food, the body, blood, soul and divinity of Christ.*

Close your prayers with
      Our Father, Hail Mary, Glory Be, Save them from the fires of hell. Amen.

Dr. Paul J. Young

Education:

California State University, Fresno, B.A in English

Dallas Theological Seminary, Th.M (Masters in Theology)

Biola University, Doctor of Ministry with emphasis on psychology (working with Talbot School of Theology, Rosemead School of Psychology and other schools)

Dr. Paul Joseph Young

Who is Dr. Paul Joseph Young?

Dr. Young, a former Evangelical Protestant pastor and leader, has been a Catholic since 1999. While a Protestant, he helped grow one of the largest high school youth programs in the nation, a group numbering 400 wild, exciting and responsive kids.

He then moved to Fort Worth, Texas where he became pastor of a small church of 200. Within nine years it became one of the largest churches in the Dallas Fort Worth area, with thousands coming to worship God. Over 50% of the growth were new converts who came into a living relationship with Jesus Christ.

From there, Dr. Young became CEO of CBS International, an in-depth bible study movement that grew from a few countries to over 60 countries in the world with thousands of people studying the Holy Scriptures in over 40 languages. It was during this ministry, traveling the world, that Dr. Young became Catholic. You can read his conversion story in the companion guide to the novel he wrote, *Lethal Discord.*

Dr. Young has planted over 90 churches throughout the world, seen over 100,000 conversions, and impacted many men and women to follow Christ. As a Catholic, he helped begin the men's ministry with Emmaus Journey, wrote *Reaching Catholic Men,* and now helps lead…

IMPAC✝MAN and IMPAC✝WOMAN

All the things accomplished by Dr. Young have only been through the strength, power and grace of God. Without Christ, Paul could have done nothing…period!

He is married to his wife and great friend, Diane. They have 5 children and 14 grandchildren. Paul and Diane lived in Santa Rosa, California for a number of years, working with their Church and Diocese and have recently moved to Freeland, WA on Whidbey Island, to be close to their son and family.

Dr. Young has been an IMPACT man most of his adult life beginning at age 15 when he started a movement on his high school campus to reach his fellow students. Soon a group of 30 grew to over 120, and a number of his buddies met around the flagpole to pray each morning before classes began.

From that day to today, Paul's drive to impact men and women has not abated.

**He wants to help you change and IMPACT
your world through praying the Rosary
for yourself, family and friends.**

Let's do it!

FREE BOOKS
FOR
YOU!

Be sure and go to <u>DrPaulYoung.com</u> and sign up for a **free book**, a book designed to take you to a new level in your walk with God.

And keep watching this site because new free books will be offered periodically.

Last, **pray for our ministry**. We are seeking to change the hearts and souls of thousands of people around the world and need your prayers. Send me a note at <u>pauljyoung@mac.com</u> if you will for this us.

Thanks, and God bless you!

OTHER BOOKS BY
DR. PAUL

1. **Lethal Discord** a Catholic Thriller. This has been called a "page turner" by many who read it. You will live the story and learn about your faith as you read this compelling novel.

2. **Lethal Discord companion guide** with questions that will help you dig deeper into the novel.

3. **Great Men of the Bible - Saint Paul, his secret to success.** The story of his success can be yours!

4. **The Personalized Bible, Philippians**
    This book will help you to make right choices about feeling great. I take the book of Philippians, a book in the New Testament, and write it as if it were written to YOU. Reading this book for 30 DAYS in a row could have a great impact on the joy you experience every day.

5. **Amazing Women of the Bible** - women you never knew before. Read this dramatic presentation of these great women! You will not be the same.

6. **Know What You Believe** - the catechism for today. A simple way to learn what you believe, a method for you and your family can use that will give you a depth of understanding of your Catholic Faith.

7. **You Can Change Your World** - a powerful book that gives us the secret to changing our world. It's explosive!

8. **How To Finish Well.** A Catholic book for Retired men who want to make the most of their retirement.

9. **Potato Salad for the Depressed Soul** - Magical steps to take to blast away depression while making potato salad! This is a crazy book that could change your life and bring the joy you are looking for.

10. **TOTAL RELIEF SYSTEMS SERIES** (3 books in each category - 9 books total). These are books written to help people overcome their emotional struggles and find peace, purpose, and joy. They take a person into an in depth journey to find restoration and healing for their souls.

- **Dr. Paul's TOTAL RELIEF** - Depression

- There are *NINE books in this series*, books that will liberate you from depression and anxiety, setting you on the pathway toward JOY, the kind of life you dreamed of.

11. **The Encyclopedia of Triggering Events.** There are so many things that happen to us with interpretations that guarantee that we feel bad. Want to change your interpretations and actions so you feel a lot better? This is a must read. It will TRAIN you to think and act right.

12. **The NOTE.** Why has the music left your soul? What is life all about? How can I get music back into your inner being, a song that fills me with hope and joy? This book is both a visual and verbal parable about the NOTE and how he can change you life…NOW!

13. **30 Days To Making Your Wife Feel Special.** This book could radically change your marriage…in only 30 days. Take the challenge. You nor your wife will be the same.

14. **If There Is A God, Whose God Is God?** Who's right, the atheists? The agnostics? What about the eastern religions, or the Jews, or Islam? And then all those Protestants…why do Catholics believe that the Church is really Catholic? Lots of questions. Lots of answers. It will be a faith-building adventure.

15. **The Unexpected Visitor.** What would happen if you opened your front door and saw Jesus standing there, wanting to come in a stay for a few days. What would you do? How would you act? Would you make any changes? This book delves into a couple who had to allow Jesus to stay with them and the changes it made in their lives.

16. **How To Be An IMPACT MAN** - a powerful book that will help men to become spiritual forces in their homes, Churches, workplaces and the world.

 *This book is also published in a young adult edition designed for college student and young single men.

17. **The IMPACT MAN** *Daily Walk* - a daily devotional for men that will take them to another level in their walk with God. It's practical and powerful! (also in a Young Adult edition).

18. **How To Be An IMPACT WOMAN** - a powerful book that will help women to become spiritual forces in their homes, Churches, workplaces and the world.

19. **The IMPACT WOMAN** *Daily Walk.* This daily read includes all the books of the bible from Genesis to Revelation with each day focusing on I.M.P.A.C.T. Reading it every day will revolutionize your life.

20. **GUARANTEED RECOVERY from a loss.** Have you lost something dear, a relative, friend, home, job, reputation or money? This book is for you. I teach a simple T.A.P. technique for overcoming loss and finding peace and joy again.

21. **Gold, Glory & Girls.** What do men want? What do they really want and need? This book takes them on a journey to the forth "G" that men need...GOD and the fulfillment that brings to their souls.

22. **I'm Praying The ROSARY for YOU!** This book will not only change your life as you pray the Rosary but will change the lives of family members and friends you pray for. You not only buy the book for yourself but buy a copy for each person you pray for and send them this personal book with their name written in it over 100 times! When a family member or friend read the prayers you are praying for them, they will, in many cases, be brought closer to God and begin to not only live out their faith, but begin to impact others too.

23. The Personalized ROSARY. You will learn how to pray the Rosary in a specific, purposeful, powerful way...just for YOU! Your life will not be the same as you pray these prayers and draw closer to our Blessed Mother and Jesus Christ our Lord.

24. How To Pray The ROSARY For Your Family. You can have great impact on your family through your prayers. The Holy Spirit will take what you pray and in obvious and subtle ways make it happen in God's time as you pray specifically with purpose and direction. This book will guide you how to pray POWERFUL PRAYERS for your family, prayers that will not only change them...but you!

Look for coming books at <u>DrPaulYoung.com</u>

A DRPAULYOUNG.COM **publication**

Making a difference now...and forever

I would appreciate if you would

give me a good review of this book.

A good review (4 or 5 stars) encourages people to

read the book and hopefully change their lives.

Thank you for taking the time to do this. Go to this book title at

amazon.com.

Made in the USA
Monee, IL
23 October 2023

45042642R00096